SUSAN B. *Anthony*

SPIRIT
of America®

Susan B. *Anthony*

REFORMER

By Cynthia Klingel and Robert B. Noyed

The
Child's
World

The Child's World®
Chanhassen, Minnesota

6

SUSAN B. *Anthony*

Published in the United States of America by The Child's World®
PO Box 326 • Chanhassen, MN 55317-0326 • 800-599-READ • www.childsworld.com

Acknowledgments
  The Child's World®: Mary Berendes, Publishing Director

  Editorial Directions, Inc.: E. Russell Primm, Emily Dolbear, and Lucia Raatma, Editors; Linda S.
  Koutris, Photo Selector; Dawn Friedman, Photo Research; Red Line Editorial, Fact Research; Irene
  Keller, Copy Editor; Tim Griffin/IndexServ, Indexer; Chad Rubel, Proofreader

Photo
  Cover: Bettmann/Corbis; Bettmann/Corbis: 2, 13 bottom, 14 top, 14 bottom, 17, 21, 23, 26; Corbis:
  27; Getty Images: 9, 28 bottom; Hulton Archive/Getty Images: 11, 13 top, 19, 25; Library of
  Congress: 6, 18, 22; North Wind Picture Archives: 7, 8, 12, 15, 20, 24; Stock Montage: 28 top.

Library of Congress Cataloging-in-Publication Data
  Klingel, Cynthia Fitterer.
    Susan B. Anthony : reformer / by Cynthia Klingel and Robert B. Noyed.
      p. cm.
  Summary: Briefly introduces the life and accomplishments of American
  social reformer Susan B. Anthony.
  Includes bibliographical references and index.
    ISBN 1-56766-171-8 (lib. bdg. : alk. paper)
  1. Anthony, Susan B. (Susan Brownell), 1820–1906—Juvenile literature.
  2. Feminists—United States—Biography—Juvenile literature.
  3. Suffragists—United States—Biography—Juvenile literature. 4. Women
  social reformers—United States—Biography—Juvenile literature.
  5. Women's rights—United States—History—Juvenile literature.
  [1. Anthony, Susan B. (Susan Brownell), 1820–1906. 2. Suffragists.
  3. Women—Biography.] I. Noyed, Robert B. II. Title.
    HQ1413.A55 K57 2002
    305.42'092—dc21

                              2001007819

14   25   26

Contents

Chapter ONE

A Quaker's Daughter

SUSAN B. ANTHONY FOUGHT HARD FOR WOMEN'S rights throughout her life. At a time when women had few rights in the United States, she wanted women to be treated equally. Her work as an American **reformer** in the 1800s helped to create greater rights for women worldwide.

Susan Brownell Anthony was born on February 15, 1820, in Adams, Massachusetts. Her parents, Daniel and Lucy Anthony, had six children. Daniel owned a small cotton mill. Lucy took care of their children as well as the girls who worked in the mill and boarded in their home. Women or girls operated all the looms in the mill.

Susan B. Anthony was born in this house in Adams, Massachusetts, in 1820.

6

Susan's father was a **Quaker**, and he was stern with his children. He wanted his children to realize their worth. He also believed in treating his daughters with as much respect as his sons. Quakers believed that boys and girls should have the same chance to learn.

Susan was a very bright child. She could read and write when she was only three years old! When Susan was six, the family moved to Battenville, New York. Her father was going to manage a larger mill there.

Girls operated all the looms in the Anthony family's mill.

Susan started school in Battenville. When the teacher refused to teach Susan long division, her father removed her from the school. He started his own school and hired Mary Perkins as the teacher. Having a woman teacher showed Susan and her sisters that women could do a variety of important jobs.

Many of the girls who worked at the cotton mill lived with the Anthony family. Susan had to help her mother with the housework. Susan and her sisters had to cook, clean, sew,

Many mills, such as these beside the river in Lowell, Massachusetts, were in operation when Susan B. Anthony was young.

wash, and iron. They also took care of the garden and the chickens. Very little time was left for play or fun.

When Susan was 12 years old, her father needed someone to help at the cotton mill. She begged her father to let her work at the mill. Her father agreed to let her work for two weeks. Susan saved the money she earned to buy a set of cups and saucers for her mother. She was very proud to give her mother that special gift.

When Susan was 17 years old, her father lost the mill. The family needed money, so Susan went to work to help out. In those days, few jobs existed for women. Susan found work, however, as a teacher.

8

She was a very smart and friendly young woman and she enjoyed people. Many men admired Susan, and at least one asked her to marry him, but she turned him down. In those days, women had no rights under the law. Women were often treated as property rather than like people. If she married, Susan would not have been allowed to keep anything she owned or any money she earned. Her husband would have had control over her. Susan did not like that idea, so she never married.

Susan B. Anthony worked as a schoolteacher.

Anthony earned about two dollars a week as a teacher. She was paid much less than a man was paid for the same work. When she complained about how little she was paid, she was fired. Then she became principal of a girls' school in Rochester, New York. After more than 10 years as a teacher, she began trying to improve social issues.

QUAKERS ARE MEMBERS OF A CHRISTIAN CHURCH CALLED THE Religious Society of Friends. An Englishman named George Fox founded Quakerism in about 1647.

In early America, white men held the good jobs, got the better educations, and made many decisions for their families and the country. The Quakers believed in the equality of men and women, however. In their homes and communities, women had the same rights as men. Girls received the same education as the boys. Like the men, Quaker girls and women had jobs. Also, Quakers did not believe in slavery.

The Quakers have always believed in settling arguments peacefully. They do not believe in fighting, especially with weapons. They do not support war.

Today, the Quaker people look for peaceful ways to change laws. They are often involved in efforts to help others who are in need. They work to make life better for people of all cultures and countries.

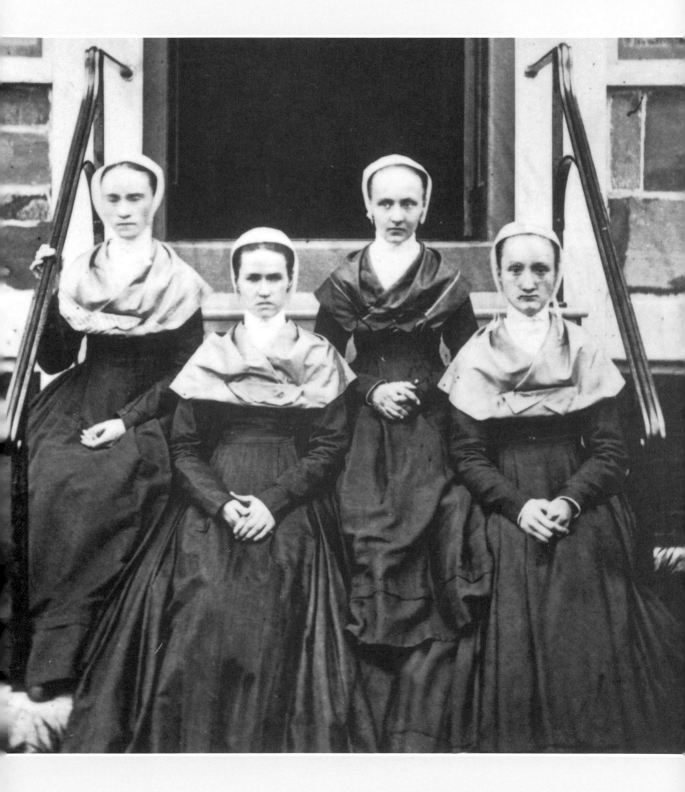

Chapter TWO

More Work to Do

IN 1849, SUSAN B. ANTHONY STOPPED TEACHING. She began to focus on two important social problems of that time. Many people were concerned about slavery. As a Quaker, Anthony was opposed to slavery. She decided to join the antislavery movement.

Susan B. Anthony worked to end slavery in the United States.

After Anthony began working to end slavery, she met Frederick Douglass. A former slave, Douglass was now an **abolitionist**. An abolitionist is someone who worked to outlaw slavery before the Civil War (1861–1865). Anthony attended many of Douglass's speeches about ending slavery.

Susan B. Anthony was also interested in the **temperance** movement. The temperance movement was organized to reduce—and later ban—

alcohol use. Anthony knew many women who had been hurt or beaten by drunken men. She wanted to stop this.

Anthony began attending the meetings of a group called the Sons of Temperance. The group was made up mostly of men. Because she was a woman, Anthony was not allowed to speak at the meetings. As a result, she started her own organization, called

Amelia Bloomer

Elizabeth Cady Stanton and Susan B. Anthony in a photograph from about 1881

the Woman's State Temperance Society of New York. It was the first such organization started by a woman.

She also began writing articles about temperance for a newspaper called *The Lily*. It was probably the first newspaper in the United States edited by a woman—Amelia Jenks Bloomer. In time, Susan B. Anthony met other women interested in the abolition movement.

Many people who supported abolition were also interested in woman **suffrage**. These people wanted to improve women's rights. One of these women was Elizabeth Cady Stanton.

Susan B. Anthony met Stanton at a temperance meeting in 1851. The two shared an interest in improving the rights of women in the United States. They began to organize the women's movement in the United States. Stanton and Anthony became life-long friends.

Anthony gave many speeches about women's rights. She organized several state and national **conventions** on the issue. In the state of New York, Susan B. Anthony organized a **petition** that would give women the right to vote and own property. Many people signed the petition. In 1860, the New York state government approved the Married Women's Property Act, which allowed women to keep their own property and their own wages.

Susan B. Anthony continued to work on the temperance, antislavery, and women's rights movements. She had already become an important leader. But she had much more work to do.

A leader in the temperance, antislavery, and women's rights movements, Susan B. Anthony (right) spoke to many audiences.

Elizabeth Cady Stanton

ELIZABETH CADY STANTON WAS AN EARLY LEADER OF THE women's rights movement. She was born Elizabeth Cady on November 12, 1815, in Johnstown, New York. She studied books in her father's law office and learned many things that most girls of that time did not know.

Elizabeth Cady Stanton was opposed to slavery. She was also unhappy with the way women were treated in the United States. They had no rights and could make no decisions for themselves. In 1840, she married an abolitionist leader named Henry B. Stanton. In time, she would give birth to seven children.

In 1848, Elizabeth Cady Stanton helped organize the first national convention for women's rights. She convinced women to stand up for their rights. In 1869, Stanton and Susan B. Anthony formed the National Woman Suffrage Association.

For more than 50 years, Elizabeth Cady Stanton worked for the rights of women. She was an excellent speaker and writer. Many of the rights women have today are the result of the courage and hard work of leaders such as Elizabeth Cady Stanton. She died in New York City on October 26, 1902.

Chapter THREE

Rights for Women

In this political cartoon, Susan B. Anthony chases President Grover Cleveland, who is carrying a book called What I Know about Women's Clubs *while Uncle Sam laughs in the background.*

AS SUSAN B. ANTHONY CONTINUED TO WORK for equal rights for all, women's rights became her most important goal. She and Elizabeth Cady Stanton worked hard to make a difference. They worked well together. Stanton was the thinker and writer. Anthony was the organizer. She thought up **strategies** for the movement.

Susan B. Anthony also made many of the public appearances. She gave many of the speeches. As a result, Anthony was the one who was criticized. Newspapers published nasty cartoons about her.

About this time, a new type of women's clothing was introduced. It was a loose, comfortable skirt worn over loose trousers gathered at the ankles. In those days, women usually wore tight, uncomfortable dresses. The skirts were often big and clumsy. These new pants were named after another woman fighting for women's rights—the *Lily* editor Amelia Jenks Bloomer.

Most women were afraid to wear bloomers. They didn't want people to think they were improperly dressed. Anthony decided bloomers were great to wear on her travels, however. But when she gave a speech, people paid more attention to her clothes than to her words. She decided to stop wearing bloomers.

Susan B. Anthony was a convincing speaker. But many people—both men and women—were angry about her message. They still did not believe in women's rights. And they did not agree that African-Americans should be free from slavery or have civil rights. They thought Anthony was not acting the way a woman should. People criticized her, and some even threw rotten eggs at her!

Named after Amelia Jenks Bloomer, the reformer, bloomers were loose trousers for women.

Interesting Fact

▶ Frederick Douglass, a famous former slave, attended the first women's rights convention in 1848. He became an honorary member of the group.

19

In 1865, the House of Representatives passes the 13th Amendment, outlawing slavery in the United States.

But Anthony would not give up. Finally, in 1865, the U.S. government passed the 13th **Amendment** to the U.S. **Constitution**. This amendment outlawed slavery in the United States. All the slaves were now free. The slaves could not own property or vote, however. And they still had no rights. For African-Americans, Susan B. Anthony's work was not yet done.

At this time, however, the rights of women had even less support than the rights of black people. Many people who had supported Anthony were now speaking out only for the rights of African-American men. Anthony had to refocus her efforts on women's rights. She

20

traveled around the United States persuading people to sign a petition. This petition asked the U.S. government to give American women the right to vote.

In 1868, the states approved another important amendment to the Constitution. The 14th Amendment gave protection to people in the United States without giving African-Americans or women the right to vote. Anthony was very disappointed. It seemed as though all her hard work had made no difference. She knew that to continue the fight, she would have to start all over again.

After the Civil War, former slaves, such as these in the South, were able to vote.

Chapter FOUR

"Failure Is Impossible"

*A photograph of an
older Susan B. Anthony*

SUSAN B. ANTHONY MADE UP HER MIND TO
continue the fight for women's rights. In 1868,
she began publishing a paper called *The
Revolution*. Its purpose was to convince people
to give women the right to vote
and to pay women and men the
same wages for the same work.

Then, in 1869, she helped
form the Working Women's
Association. That same year, she
and Elizabeth Cady Stanton formed
a group called the National Woman
Suffrage Association. The paper
and the group were so outspoken,
however, that even some women
who agreed with their ideas were
afraid to join.

During this time, Anthony did not travel or give speeches often. But after a couple of years, *The Revolution* had lost so much money that Anthony had to stop publishing it. She began traveling again and giving speeches. She had to earn money to pay off the bills from *The Revolution*.

In 1870, the states approved the 15th Amendment. It gave African-American men the right to vote. Again, nothing had changed for women.

A meeting of the National Woman Suffrage Association, formed in 1869 by Susan B. Anthony and Elizabeth Cady Stanton

Interesting Fact

▶ Susan B. Anthony helped raise funds to pay for the admission of women to the University of Rochester in 1900.

The 15th Amendment, passed in 1870, gave African-American men the right to vote.

Anthony wondered about new strategies for the movement. She thought about the language of the 14th Amendment passed in 1868. She talked to lawyers. Then she had an idea. The amendment said that no state shall "deprive any person of life, liberty, or property." It did not say that these rights were only for men. She decided to test her idea. She would vote!

24

On November 5, 1872, Susan B. Anthony and 15 other women became the first women to vote in a U.S. election. Three weeks later, all the women were arrested for breaking the law. Soon, all the women were released, except Anthony. She had to remain in jail until her court appearance.

At her trial, the jury found Susan B. Anthony guilty. It is believed that the judge told the jury to find Anthony guilty. After the jury gave their decision, the judge fined her $100, which was a lot of money at that time. Anthony refused to pay it. To avoid revealing the unfairness of the trial, the judge took no further action against her. Susan B. Anthony was now a hero for many people.

The National American Woman Suffrage Association staged many marches, such as this one in New York City.

Susan B. Anthony at her desk in 1898

Finally, many women and men were listening to what Susan B. Anthony was saying. In the following years, Anthony and Stanton accomplished several things. They published a set of books called *History of Woman Suffrage*. In 1890, their National Woman Suffrage Association merged with another group to form the National American Woman Suffrage Association. Some states even passed laws giving women more rights. But women still could not vote.

Susan B. Anthony was now 80 years old, but she had not lost her energy or her passion for what she believed. She continued to speak out as a social reformer until her death on March 13, 1906. In her last speech, she inspired the audience with the words, "Failure is impossible."

After her death, Susan B. Anthony left a group of people committed to what she believed. In 1920—14 years later—the states approved the 19th Amendment, finally giving women in the United States the right to vote.

In 1922, women in New York City vote in their first federal election after passage of the 19th Amendment.

THE 19TH AMENDMENT WAS FIRST proposed in Congress in 1878. It took many years and much hard work to pass the amendment that gave women in the United States the right to vote (right).

Supporters of the amendment around the country tried to convince the U.S. government and citizens in many ways. They worked hard to get states to give women the right to vote. They held parades and organized hunger strikes. They even filed lawsuits challenging laws that allowed only men to vote. Some opponents of the 19th Amendment harassed and even jailed supporters of woman suffrage.

Sixty-sixth Congress of the United States of America;

At the First Session,

Begun and held at the City of Washington on Monday, the nineteenth day of May, one thousand nine hundred and nineteen.

JOINT RESOLUTION

Proposing an amendment to the Constitution extending the right of suffrage to women.

Resolved by the Senate and House of Representatives of the United States of America in Congress assembled (two-thirds of each House concurring therein), That the following article is proposed as an amendment to the Constitution, which shall be valid to all intents and purposes as part of the Constitution when ratified by the legislatures of three-fourths of the several States.

"ARTICLE ———.

"The right of citizens of the United States to vote shall not be denied or abridged by the United States or by any State on account of sex.

"Congress shall have power to enforce this article by appropriate legislation."

F. H. Gillett

Speaker of the House of Representatives.

Thos. R. Marshall

Vice President of the United States and President of the Senate.

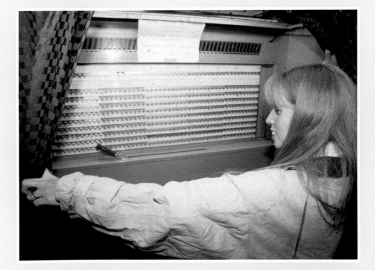

The 19th Amendment was finally approved on August 10, 1920. Today, on Election Day, women across the United States are able to express their wishes in voting booths (left) alongside men. The 19th Amendment is often known as the "Susan B. Anthony Amendment" as a tribute to the reformer.

Time LINE

1820　　1869　　2000s

1820 Susan Brownell Anthony is born in Adams, Massachusetts, on February 15.

1826 The Anthony family moves to Battenville, New York.

1838 After Daniel Anthony loses his cotton mill in Battenville, Susan B. Anthony starts working as a teacher.

1849 Susan B. Anthony decides to end her career as teacher to join the temperance movement.

1860 After Anthony's campaigning, the New York legislature approves the Married Women's Property Act.

1865 The U.S. government passes the 13th Amendment to the Constitution, outlawing slavery in the country.

1868 Anthony begins publishing a women's rights newspaper called *The Revolution.*

1869 Anthony helps form the Working Women's Association. She and Elizabeth Cady Stanton establish the National Woman Suffrage Association.

1872 On November 5, Susan B. Anthony and others become the first women to vote in a U.S. election. Three weeks later, they are arrested for breaking the law. Anthony never pays the $100 fine she is ordered to pay.

1881 Anthony and Stanton start work on a set of books called *History of Woman Suffrage.*

1890 Anthony and Stanton's National Woman Suffrage Association merges with another group to form the National American Woman Suffrage Association.

1906 Susan B. Anthony dies on March 13 in Rochester, New York.

29

Glossary Terms

abolitionist (ab-uh-LISH-uh-nist)
An abolitionist is someone who worked to outlaw slavery before the Civil War (1861–1865). Frederick Douglass was a leading abolitionist.

amendment (uh-MEND-muhnt)
An amendment is a change or addition to the U.S. Constitution or any other legal document. The 13th Amendment outlawed slavery in the United States in 1865.

constitution (kon-stuh-TOO-shuhn)
A constitution is a set of basic principles used to govern a state, country, or society. The 13th Amendment to the U.S. Constitution was passed in 1865.

conventions (kuhn-VEN-shuns)
Conventions are large gatherings of people with similar interests. Susan B. Anthony organized many women's rights conventions during her lifetime.

petition (puh-TISH-uhn)
A petition is a request signed by many people asking leaders to change a policy or action. In the 1850s, Susan B. Anthony organized a petition to give women the right to vote and own property.

Quaker (KWAY-kur)
A Quaker is a member of the Religious Society of Friends, a Christian group that holds simple religious services, wears plain clothes, and opposes war. Susan B. Anthony's father was a Quaker.

reformer (re-FORM-er)
A reformer is someone who tries to improve a law, custom, or practice. Susan B. Anthony was a reformer who worked to improve women's rights.

strategies (STRAT-uh-jeez)
Strategies are clever plans. Susan B. Anthony and others had to develop many strategies to win over people to their plans for equality for women.

suffrage (SUHF-rij)
Suffrage is the right to vote. The woman suffrage movement worked to give women the right to vote.

temperance (TEM-pur-enss)
The temperance movement was an organized effort to reduce, and later ban, alcohol use. Susan B. Anthony was a member of the temperance movement.

For Further INFORMATION

Web Sites

Visit our homepage for lots of links about Susan B. Anthony:
http://www.childsworld.com/links.html

Note to Parents, Teachers, and Librarians:
We routinely verify our Web links to make sure they're safe,
active sites—so encourage your readers to check them out!

Books

Isaacs, Sally Senzell. *America in the Time of Susan B. Anthony: The Story of Our Nation from Coast to Coast.* Chicago, Ill.: Heinemann Library, 2001.

Kendall, Martha E. *Susan B. Anthony: Voice for Women's Voting Rights.* Springfield, N.J.: Enslow Publishers, Inc., 1997.

Levin, Pamela. *Susan B. Anthony: Fighter for Women's Rights.* New York: Chelsea House, 1993.

Parker, Barbara Keevil. *Susan B. Anthony: Daring to Vote.* Brookfield, Conn.: Millbrook Press, 1998.

Places to Visit or Contact

The Susan B. Anthony House
To visit the home of the legendary American civil rights leader
17 Madison Street
Rochester, NY 14608
585-235-6124

Women's Rights National Historical Park
To find out more about the history of women's rights
136 Fall Street
Seneca Falls, NY 13148
315-568-2991

Index